access to the silence

A lot of hard work by everyone involved went into the production of this book but as happens a gremlin crept in and assembly appears as assembley on p30.

TL

Tom Leonard: Previous Publications

Six Glasgow Poems, Other People Publications, Glasgow 1969

A Priest Came on at Merkland Street, Midnight Press, Glasgow 1970

Poems, E. & T. O'Brien, Dublin 1973

Bunnit Husslin, Third Eye Centre, Glasgow 1975

Three Glasgow Writers (with Alex Hamilton and James Kelman),
Molendinar Press, Glasgow 1976

My Name is Tom (Soundpoem score), Good Elf Press, London 1978

If Only Bunty Was Here (Radio play), Print Studio Press, Glasgow 1979

Ghostie Men, Galloping Dog Press, Newcastle 1980

Satires and Profanities (Political Revue Pieces),
Scottish Trades Union Congress, Glasgow 1984

Intimate Voices: Selected Work 1965-1983, Galloping Dog Press, Newcastle1984;
republished Vintage, London 1995; etruscan books, Devon 2003

Situations Theoretical and Contemporary, Galloping Dog Press, Newcastle 1986

Two Members' Monologues and *A Handy Form for Artists for Use in Connection with The City of Culture*, The Edward Polin Press, Glasgow 1989

nora's place, Galloping Dog Press, Newcastle 1990

On the Mass Bombing of Iraq and Kuwait, Commonly Known As "the Gulf War" with
Leonard's Shorter Catechism, AK Press, Stirling 1991

Places of the Mind: The Life and Work of James Thomson ('B.V.'), Cape, London 1993

A Letter in Reply to a Request for a Poem for a Poems for Bosnia *anthology, 'in which* The Independent *has an interest'*, Infolio, Cambridge 1994

Reports from the Present, Cape, London 1995

Etruscan Reader V (with Bill Griffiths and Tom Raworth), etruscan books, Devon 1997

inside looking in, Survivors Press, Glasgow 2004

As editor:

Radical Renfrew: Poetry from the French Revolution to the First World War,
Polygon, Edinburgh 1990

Tom Leonard

access to the silence

poems and posters 1984-2004

etruscan books
2004

access to the silence

First published by etruscan books 2004

etruscan books
28 Fowlers Court, Fore Street
Buckfastleigh
South Devonshire TQ11 0AA

<etruscan@macunlimited.net>
www.e-truscan.co.uk

ISBN 1 901538 47 8
ISBN 1 901538 48 6 (cased)
Twenty-six copies of *access to the silence* are cased and lettered A-Z by the author with an additional hand written text.

etruscan books are distributed in America by SPD, 1341 7th Street, Berkeley CA, 94710 <orders@spdbooks.org>, and are available in Australia from Collected Works, 1st Floor, Flinders Way Arcade, 238 Flinders Lane, Melbourne 3000.

Funded by The Arts Council

etruscan books are edited by Nicholas Johnson
Cover by Sonya Leonard
Typography by R.W. Palmer, Tuff Talk Press, Bath
<robertw.palmer@tiscali.co.uk>
Printed at Angel Press, Gateshead, Tyne and Wear

ARTS COUNCIL ENGLAND

ACKNOWLEDGEMENTS
Some of this work appeared first in two booklets from Galloping Dog Press, in *Reports From The Present* (Cape), Etruscan Reader V (etruscan books), The London Review of Books, the Edinburgh Review, Lines Review, PN Review, Peacock Blue, Ink Feathers, e.r.v (1st edn.), Gare du Nord, Boxkite and Salisbury Festival poem fireworks display.
'Blessed Trinity' was produced as a silkscreen print by Euan Sutherland in an edition of 50.

NOTE: The final paragraph of "Ach Caledonia" is from Grotowski, *Towards a Poor Theatre,* Methuen, 1969, p.89.

CONTENTS

100 Differences Between Poetry and Prose

poetry stops before the end of the margin
you can talk about prose without mentioning school
you don't read poetry to get from Glasgow to Saltcoats without noticing

John Menzies doesn't stock poetry
whoever heard of war & peace having the line as a unit of semantic yield
you can call a poem what you want and say it's poetic licence

poetry is the subliminal history of linguistic shape
ahem
poetry has four wheels, two wings and a pair of false teeth

poetry is the heart and the brain divided by the lungs
poetry is the world's oldest cock and fanny story

you don't get prose in anapaestic dimeters
nobody publishes their first slim volume of prose
aristotle never wrote The Proses

if you dribble past five defenders, it isn't called sheer prose
poets are the unacknowledged thingwaybobs

poetry is quintessentially contrapuntal
the square root of poetry is an ever-evolving quark
whenever Vergil looked in the mirror, he beheld an epic Latin poet

poetry is all the juicy bits in the juiciest order
poetry is jellied religion
pascal: if your labourers complain too much, try taking them to a poetry reading

prose goes scchhpludd
prose goes scchhpludd scchhpludd clomp clomp clomp
are you sitting comfortably

then I'll end

The Evidence
(Sheriff Court: Glasgow, April 1995)

I gave chase
to the appellant
with his bucket and billposters

and he fell, my lord,
on the point of my apprehending
him. At which point

I too fell down
– we had come to a grassy slope –
and coming to, I found

the appellant lying
with a bloodied face
on the adjacent path.

My colleague constable lindsay
who had herself fallen down
in the chase, saw nothing of this:

but she arrived in time to find
myself and the appellant
lying some feet apart.

That witness was lying
who said I stood over Mr Anwar
and kicked him where he lay;

nor did I tell the appellant:
"This is what happens
to black boys with big mouths."

The truth is that I felt sorry for him,
so I called an ambulance,
which I boarded with my colleague

and therein charged the appellant
under the Environment Protection Act, Scotland,
with the illegal posting of bills.

proem

who are we, trapped in our ways
                    of dying towards the fact
of only once having been, together

or separate in our own being
            but never wholly separate, only a part
of the time we live in, and with others occupy

(1)

who wants to be free
who has need of air

who is changing

who has a different definition
who has no definition

instance
(the right)

who wants to find out what it is
who wants to go forward

who wants to

(2)

your eyes

the iris grey or is it green
the blue iris

we both love
safely, using the word

and the freschia
with the smell of freschia

filling the room
coming home,
surprised

that place we share

An Ageing Writer

The early angular anger
is now
an avuncular geniality;

the early humour,
– an earnestness of poise.

It's difficult to stay angry
on a full belly;

– difficult to stay funny
on a bitterly swallowed pill.

epitaph

you forced open the door
for the trapped

who broke through
shouting

out of the way
half-opener of doors

AN OXFORD DICTIONARY OF AN ENGLISH LANGUAGE

An Old Story

They invented the concept, and then they invented the concept of their own ownership, of it. They invented the institutions from within which they lent out things to see if others could replicate their fitness-to-own. Fitness to own, they said, resided in the ability to say why and how a thing was or was not a thing-within-the-concept. Only things-within-the-concept had value within the institutions. In owning the concept, they owned the things-within-the-concept, and made their living by them.

They said silly things like, "When we speak of greatness in a literary work we normally do so because we recognise that it has enlarged our knowledge of the nature and capacities of man." By "we" they pretended to mean the whole human race, but really they meant people like themselves who in owning the things-within-the-concept, conceptually owned that which contained the values of the whole human race, in their own terms. From within the institutions they were thus not merely members of the human race, but conceptual owners of its values. This made them feel good.

A maker of a thing was not necessarily a maker of a thing-within-the-concept, and was certainly not an owner of the concept, unless in that separate institutional capacity alone. The maker in his being as a human was only part of that whole human race whose values the owners-of-the-concept conceptually owned. Yet the owners of the concept might choose to make public, or privately to reveal to the maker, any added store of knowedge of the nature and capacities of man, which the maker's made-thing had disclosed. Thus the makers would come to know their place in the Great Chain of Being.

Their place was supposedly within the word owned by the owners of the concept: for the concept was the enclosing word, and ownership of that word had been, and always would be, the irreconcileable opposite.

a
parasite that
survives by
defining the host
in ways that
maintain its own
habitat

the
institution
of the
state

sequence:

HESITATIONS

monologues for dancing

for Jim Ferguson

so whut day yi day yi yirsell then ih

whut day yi day these days

* *

really
been a while intit

thats good
that's   ok then ih

ahm thi same

a dont give a shite
fur any a thim

a dont give a
  a dogs turd

supposin
supposin thi entire

fuckin lot
and all thir fuckin wurks
                    an pomps

copped it
copped thi fuckin

whole thing
smack

it would serve
it would serve thim

entirely accordin
tay thaht
which they totally fuckin deserve

thats ma opinion
and having delivered it
I will now have my fucking breakfast

same time yi wunnir
least ah day

yi surta
keep trynti avoid it thats
the difficult bitty it

jist
no keep findn yirsell
sitn

wotchn thi telly ur
lookn oot thi windy

that wey yi say
christ a could

go a roll n egg
ur
whuts thi time fuck me

wiv nay
cookn oil nwi need
potatoes

seen im? seen im?

other times though

fuckin murder eh

couldny turn a

christ ah.
a mean

yup

if bit

nah its

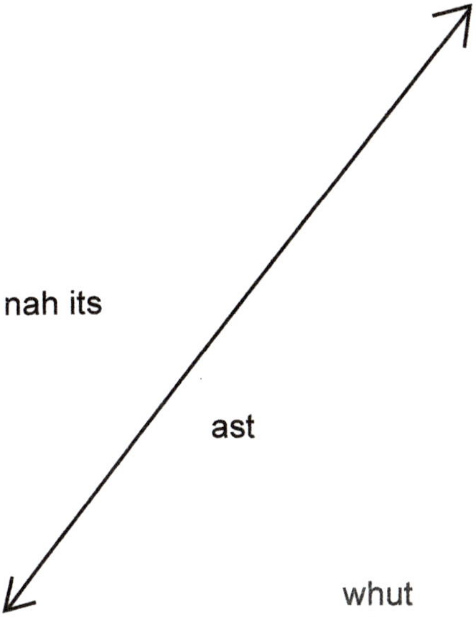

ast

whut
whut

thi wey she wuz last time

that wey

if its

m ach

n

p

o

. obl

f

ih

t

s

if

paw

s

ih

if

its

oOr Kit godrestur

oOr Kit

yi

maybe

cz

how?

dont be ridiculous!

it

m

a tellt yi that

aw?

ih

nah

p

wull it
wull it

dont you believe it
no if yiv
no if yiv
                    any sense

a widny
nut a bit uv it
                                naw

no way
                     nah its

loada shite frankly
thats thi

thats thi beginnin middle n end ay it

* *

nah
its not fur me

the question does not arise
the fuckin orthodoxy of thi bastard is irrefutable

its ehm
well

a matter for thi triumvirate, one opines

itll just huv tay be
thaht wey coz it

canny be any other wey
thi noo.   no

fur thi moment.
coorss yi might find

that thingzl change—
theyll change

yon wey thit
yi didny notice

it thi time. bit
yill look back

an mine thi wey
it wuz.

n thats whin yill
sayti yirsell

well

a nivir thote ahd see thi day

(end of sequence)

Before the 1820 rising in the West of Scotland a network of

don't call them government spies

call them MI5
call them MI6
call them special branch
call them the anti-terrorist squad
call them F1, F2, F3, F4, F5, F6 right through to 12
call them counter-insurgency

don't mention them
keep quiet about them
refuse to discuss how much money's spent
refuse to discuss what they do
swear everyone to secrecy

call them Intelligence

call the critics "unpatriotic"
call the critics "a security risk"
call the critics "conspiracy theorists"
call the critics "traitors"

call the critics *paranoid*

government spies kept watch over the Combination Acts against assembley

doon the close
oot the back door

roon thi
back a thi middens

heh maw
ah shouts heh maw

gonny chuck uz doon
wan a yoan

kitsch kailyard
iconographic

jeelie pieces

ahm clean oota
kitsch kailyard

iconographic
jeelie pieces

shi shouts

flingin doon
the empty jeely jawr

she used tay
get inty the pictures wi

another of life's little canters

fuck 'im—
his vanity stood in the path
of seeing "as others see us":

so

what was not goose for the gander
was sufficient unto his own judgement

to wit—
it ain't about me
what the fuck yi beefin about?

firmly

It would be wrong not to say
this is what happened. But

considering all other points of view
as not totally invalid in themselves;

it might be safer to say nothing
about the whole incident, and

rest assured that whatever you or I
may think of it, the matter is closed.

Opting for early retirement

time only/
time management

reified agency
of cost-function conscience

numerical value
constantly

defining the scope
of being-in-the-structure

taboo being
unpredictable being

being as quantum
being as inefficient

motor tasks
establishing targets

recognising actual deficiencies
establishing potential deficiencies

guilty until innocent
the human as an agent of deficiency

the question always
and the answer always

surely total innocence is impossible

Skills

inventing jobs
teaching the skills

of applying for jobs

----

one of millions
training

to acquire the skills
to apply for jobs

-----

not out of a job
but training

to apply for a job
and to be in a job

efficiently

----

co-operating with management
competing with colleagues

learning the ropes

The underfunder's utopia

the state hospital
with one bed

always full
always efficient

Myths in these Parts

They say in these parts

"When you die,
you go to your granny's."

Your granny sits in the sky
with a bag of white peppermint lumps.

"Come on in," she says,
"You made an awful fuss of it.

We were wondering
when you were coming to see us."

respite in the reading

stepping into that space
out of the past
surrounding
this place, become
an accompanying darkness;

the role, a model
of being oneself, helped
by the places you were
led into, of your own accord.

it never changes, always
changing, this present
become a welcoming
familiar, no time to stay.

for the keeper of the journal

hoovering-up the to-be words
acquisitor, predator:
leaning through the moment
pen in hand, pen in mind;
always potential.

colonialist:
namer hungry-for-the-fame-of-naming;
the gap between being
and being-a-writer
would-be closed up.

you would become
the behaviour pattern
of your own choosing
—as if not of your choosing.

respectable rapist,
dialogue always tangential
to that unstated monologue
of your discourse with the future.

the enemy without

bomb them, bomb them!
cries
the editor of the *Catholic Herald*

through a hubbub of clichés
about "appeasement"
"if we had sat back while Hitler"

etc etc etc
the usual

the usual moral outrage

assessments of topography
linked-up tacticians
named & numbered weaponry

– only the demons have changed;

2 a.m.
in a territory without a valid state

where the journalists validate the politicians
and the politicians validate the journalists

listening to the radio
headphoned like an airpilot

while my wife sleeps by my side

MISSILES LAUNCHED FROM MORAL HIGH GROUND

THE PRESS

as

bogus phatic communion

let's not pretend it's dialogue!

ACH CALEDONIA

Notes to accompany a performance tape.

[In the mid-seventies I made a number of works for taperecorder, some to be performed with added songs and words, and the holding up of placards. The first of these *My Name is Tom* was published as a soundscore by Good Elf Press in London in 1978. *Ach Caledonia* was composed in 1975. What follows is not a description of the tape itself but a description of what took place alongside the tape when *Ach Caledonia* was being performed. The tape featured a number of different "voices" and registers, saying "Ach" in different ways, "how day ye spell it", "ma mammy's doon it the laundry", "discipline! discipline!", "not before time", Scottish country dance music mixed in with a piano version of *The Rite of Spring*, and a woman describing a restaurant where you could get a pot of tea with four cups of tea in it, breast of chicken the size of your hand, etc. The tape lasts just under 6 minutes. - T.L.]

The placards used during this work are as follows: –

a) T I C K L Y   M I N C E

b) A   B L U E   S K Y

c) A   D E A F   E G G

d) O V E R

e) A   D I E T I N G   K E T T L E D R U M

f) T H E   N E W S   O F   T H E   M U F F I N

g) T U M U L T U O U S   C E N T I P E D E S !

h) C E L T I C
1. THE WHORE OF BABYLON (OUR HOLY MOTHER THE CHURCH)
2. SENSUOUS RITES
3. INSISTENT DEPENDENCE

i) R A N G E R S
1. THE OLD TESTAMENT GOD
2. AUSTERITY
3. INSISTENT INDEPENDENCE

j)

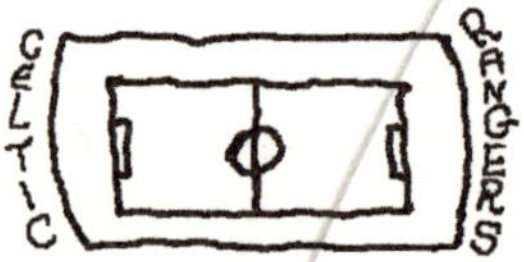

OEDIPUS SCREWING HIS MOTHER
AT BOTH ENDS

k) T H E   C O N C E P T   O F   B A T M A N

l) T H E   R E N A I S S A N C E   O F
T H E   P O K E Y - H A T

m) T H E   E X I L E   O F   T H E
V O M I T I N G   D A N D E L I O N

n) M O H N   J I L T O N

o) M R S   D A L E ' S   B R E W E R Y

p) D E L I R I U M   T R E M E N S
O F   T H E   O S T R O C C O P U S

(*Soon after tape starts, narrator reads*:)

O Caledonia! stern and wild,
Meet nurse for a poetic child!
Land of brown heath and shaggy wood,
Land of the mountain and the flood,
Land of my sires! what mortal hand
Can e'er untie the filial band,
That knits me to thy rugged strand!

(*Placard sequence* a,b,c,d. *Then begins telling quickly:*)

well as I said to Tom

Let's be honest. Let's talk about a language,
I mean a sound-system, a Glasgow sound-system,
though Belfast has similar features. Let's talk
about kinetics, e.g.–

Man: – Ma mammaizdoonit thi lawndry
Woman: – Ma maaaaaamaiz doonit thi lawwwwwwndry

(*Placards e,f,g held up.*)

Right? That's where the tactiles are at, often. The
man uppercuts, the woman clings. Let's talk about
the body, let's talk about the church, let's talk
about the bevvy. AND the industrial revolution.

well as I said to Tom

Let's be honest. Sin = sex = shame of the body,
and: –

1. Posh people use their bodies, eyebrows and things, while talking.
2. Bodies are sexual.

∴ 3. Posh people communicate sexually while talking

∴ 4. Posh people are poofs and cissies.

or why do you think we've so many doctors and

engineers? OK? A computer could have predicted
R.D.Laing, fifty years ago. Glasgow's
instant existentialism! Boom boom.
well as I said to Tom

Take the molecular family, and that. The father
as moral arbiter. But. Father O'Leary and the
Old Testament God. Both upped and snipped
the molecular father's balls. PLUS. The industrial
set-up: "You wait till your father comes home!"
and, "My daddy's a plastic button-pusher!"

(*The next paragraph usually wasn't reached. Once or twice it was added somewhere:*)

So-shu churned. Sorry. Socio-economic factors,
as per – shat on, and their language. Right.
Let's talk about the bevvy, looking for mummy
at the bottom of the glass, the "dependent" personality,
the wish to be a muscular version of Frank Sinatra...

well as I said to Tom

I'll have a pint of lager, he said.

(*Football placards h,i,j held up. Then narrator reads, angrily:*)

Ah, Sun-flower! weary of time,
Who countest the steps of the Sun,
Seeking after that sweet golden clime
Where the traveller's journey is done:

Where the Youth pined away with desire,
And the pale Virgin shrouded in snow
Arise from their graves, and aspire
Where my Sun-flower wishes to go.

(*Placards k,l,m,n,o,p held up.*)

(*Then narrator in high, thin, sort of heckling Wee Free minister's voice:*)

In order that the spectator may be stimulated into self-analysis when confronted with the actor, there must be some common ground already existing in both of them, something they can either dismiss in one gesture or worship. Artaud intuitively saw myth as the dynamic centre of the theatre performance. Only Nietzsche was ahead of him in this domain. He also knew that transgression of the myth renewed its essential values and "became an element of menace which re-established the divided norms." He did not however – (wags finger) He did NOT however – take account of the fact that in our age, when all languages intermingle, the community of the theatre cannot possibly identify itself with myth, because there is no single faith. Only an act of confrontation is possible.

(*Placards a,b,c,d.*)

(end)

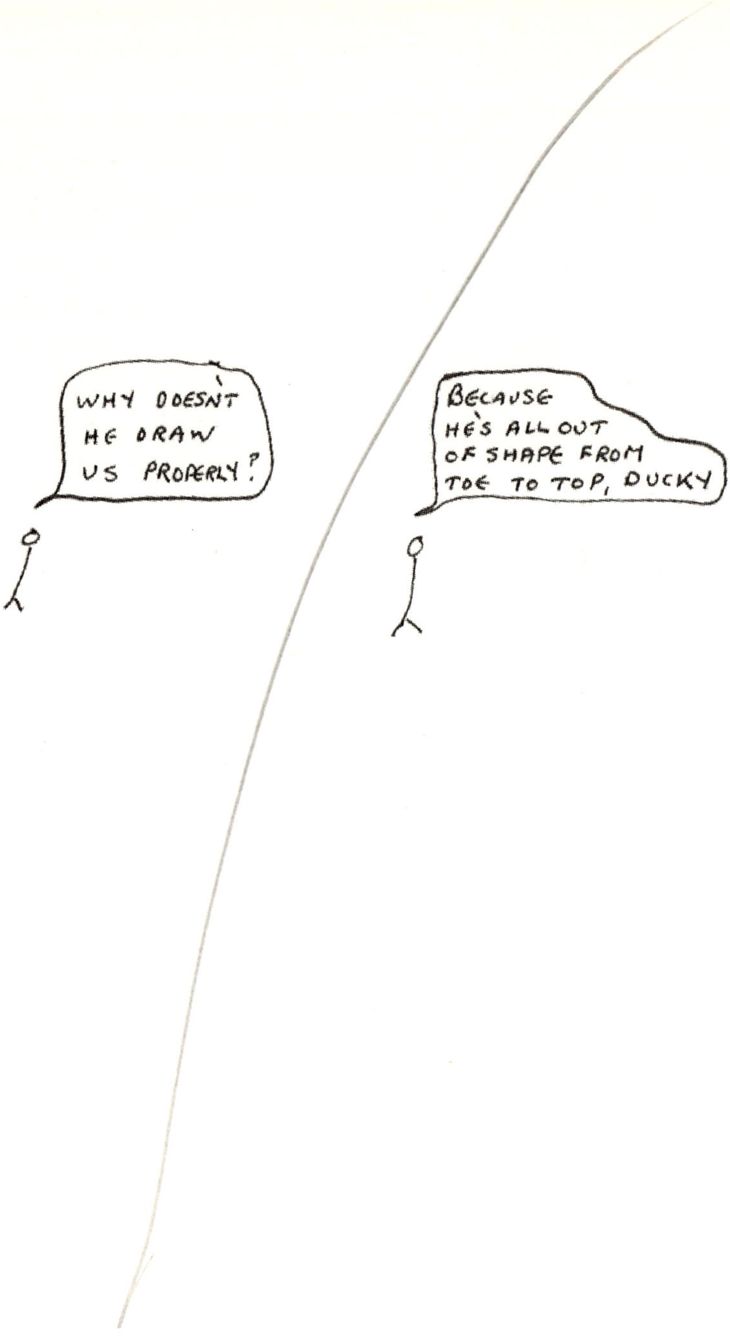
WHY DOESN'T HE DRAW US PROPERLY?
BECAUSE HE'S ALL OUT OF SHAPE FROM TOE TO TOP, DUCKY

sequence:

situations theoretical and contemporary

somewhere between stocks & shares
and the “commonsensical” editorial

pity the poor arts page
thinking itself alone

The schooner *The Mother of Parliaments* has anchored in the bay.
The first British ship has reached your land.

See the row-boat, pulling to the shore.
See the ballot-boxes, glinting in the sun!

Run and tell your fellow-tribesmen.
We are going to have a referendum!
Shall we join the British Empire?

Today is National Income Card-Carrying Day.
On this day all citizens must wear cards prominently declaring their total
income from all sources for the previous twelve months.

How full the underground shelters are this morning.
All those advocates of “tighter control of the money supply”.
And there is that expert on “international terrorism”.
Quite a card, eh?

Quick though – there goes the Chancellor of the Exchequer.
Oh dear. No pep-talk today!

You are tracing the link between existential *angst* and male sexual guilt.
From the consciousness of guilt to the guilt of consciousness.
From Dostoevsky to Sartre.

Your audience this morning is from the "Third World".
Their bodies are skeletal.
Their eyes seem very large.

One approaches the rostrum.
Food. Food.

M

Dear Member: The Party for the Political Advancement of the Upwardly Mobile Sons and Daughters of Parents who were Working Class

again requests five dead metaphors and five banal alliterations for inclusion in our party leader's keynote speech to forthcoming annual party conference:

four acceptances again guarantee admission to conference, with the opportunity to participate in the ten-minute standing ovation at the end of the speech itself.

Last year's poll-toppers, "The demise of the dreary dogmatist" and "A return to radical realism," remain eligible.

Bon appetit!

You have returned to Glasgow after a long exile.
A *Glasgow Herald* special edition is selling like hot cakes.
It publishes a Turkish poet's abstruse new song.

This Turkish poet is of an international cast of mind.
He also has an unselfconscious enjoyment of working-class culture.
In fact his song is about a match between Glasgow Celtic and Glasgow Rangers.

A certain Professor MacFadyen has detected the influence of MacDiarmid.

as I was waiting upon a bus in byres road
musing upon the *echtness* of the glasgow cultural renaissance

an elderly gentleman came walking by with a smile
who bid good morning to a woman of slightly more tender years
who smiled in reply and said

and how is the wee dog this morning mister mackay

It is five years since the edict, "Only the trauchle is clean".
Now the Inspector of Literature himself has sent his *Collected Trauchles* for review.
Grimly but morally refreshed you reach page five-hundred-and-eighty-three.

"There is not a spark of humour throughout this wholly admirable book,"
you begin your review.
"Nor has irony caused its customary obfuscation through bad faith."

The administrative resource base of school focused projects and the college-initiated curriculum in the field provides in-service whole-school comprehensive packages for the formulation, implementation and evaluation of major new initiatives developed within the time constraints appropriate to areas of deprivation. The new multi-purpose role of language across the curriculum will promote the acquisition of subject-specific concepts designed to support and underpin the implementation participation and development of supportive group structures relevant to the mutual interchange of the specific school situation in the context of the community. The conceptual structure of investigative skills will be developed in relation to the creation of dynamic self-initiated visits to explore, redefine and extend criterion-referenced modules for individual problem-solving processes. This should facilitate the co-ordination and liason of relevant core teams in providing an impetus to integrate in-service evaluation as part of the monitoring and review of inter-dependent consultancy approaches on a one-to-one basis.

The coach-driver makes an announcement.
“Your poems should have one of two titles:
‘The Vanity of Human Wishes’, or ‘There But for the Grace of God’.”

The passengers are excited.
Who will win the word processor? Will it be me?
The lights turn to green. The bus moves off at last.

Let the tour of the slums begin!

We have decided to make Scotland secure.
This is strategically essential.
No question.

Scottish people have nothing to fear.
Noise pollution should not be a problem.
And all construction work will be landscaped.

We have decided to make America secure.
This is strategically essential.
No question.

Scottish people have nothing to fear.
Noise pollution should not be a problem.
And all construction work will be landscaped.

Scotland has become an independent socialist republic.
At last.

Eh?
You pinch yourself.
Jesus Christ. You've slept in again.

And their judges spoke with one dialect,
but the condemned spoke with many voices.

And the prisons were full of many voices,
but never the dialect of the judges.

And the judges said:
"No-one is above the Law."

(end of sequence)

THE is the father

this is the holy spirit

a is the son

sequence:

nora's place

a poem in 17 aspects

across the park, walking
I can't be bothered
making the dinner, going through
all the routines and subroutines

setting it up with the radio at
four to do the peeling, work out
what the rota's been of

food this past week or so
is it time again for fish

trying to get the girls
not eat before dinner
when they come in from school

I protest at this place
with no people in it

objects for reproducing images
people not actually present

from this wall to this wall
and this wall to this wall

yes I'm all for him
becoming union rep
– don't let them get away with it!

obviously   the last settlement
was a complete sell-out
                                        but then,
aren't most union leaders like that?

on the executive, hobnobbing
far too much with managers
                              first-name terms
                              and they're always
paid far more than the worst off
who need the union most

Dives and Lazarus
that's what we agreed
last night at dinner time

soon it will be
the familiar footsteps
time   sometimes from the

bottom of the stairs the
voices drift up   maybe

if you happen to look out the window
at the right time, it is the right time

for a wave.   the wave.
people are coming home.
                                        home to

the place that has not existed
these past hours

if they're finding

the dinner school portions too wee it
must be the cutbacks that'll mean
they'd better come home at

the back of half twelve every
day I'll better maybe
keep a big pot of soup on the

go or get in some
frozen packets hamburgers
fish fingers that sort of thing

you can't give them
chips twice a day though it
wouldn't be a healthy

diet maybe I'll try to
get them go back to dinner school
take pieces with them though

to eke it out

I don't know what we share exclusively now
other than the children

the best time was when we shared the same political outlook
exclusively   but now

you've others you can do that with
the shared anger at injustice
can be had elsewhere

the main thing to have controlled
contempt for the idea of
breakdown which is completely

unromantic and painful despite
its aura and pseudo visionary crap about
insights usually obsessive petty

vanities to do with god and the
devil and one-dimensional trains
of thought that go on and on and

people don't understand you any better
at the end of it

through the
revolving turnstile
past

tomatoes
mushrooms peppers
potatoes

cheese island
milk   margarine
yoghurt

pizzas jams marmalades
beans peas carrots
pulses sauces

coffee tea
spaghetti
hoops spam tuna

salmon
ambrosia creamed rice
soups

cornflakes
all bran shredded
wheat fruit

juice soda stream
cooking oil
disposable bin liners

brillo dettol
washing soda crystals
elastoplast toothpaste

kleenex toilet rolls
soap powders fairy
liquid

dog food
birds eye codsteaks
hamburgers

frozen turkey
chicken
new zealand lamb

biscuit alley
fresh fish
on the spot baking

stand
leaning on the trolley
waiting

nora drinks too much

sometimes one beer is enough to make her go
what is it about nora's drinking

nora creates an environment in which she is approved
if she sits with drinkers, her being a drinker is approved
she is "finally approved simply for what she is"

nora is allowed out the house twice a week
nora's terms are that she doesn't sit with males
nora doesn't want to sit with males anyway
nora sits with alice and betty, who are always there

when nora gets to the Whistler's Dog, alice and betty approve of her coming

now he has an affair of the soul elsewhere
now he has the chance to be “as free as himself”
that is what it’s about, the sense to be “as free as himself”

maybe to be as free as himself, he has to have the mother at home

* * *

when will nora become herself
when will nora feel “as free as herself”

is nora “just another person”?

you get that way you get
scared to go out –
                                        don't you:

just that way that
you find yourself putting off
going to the butchers or
                                                    the newsagents;

that thing about
                                    just talking,
where do you put your eyes:
where do you put your eyes
when you're
                                    just talking?

people can tell when you're
                                    not good at it, look

surprised and a bit hurt

lying looking sideways up
at the bedside photo of my youngest

strange to see that smile
that same set of features
on the face of a woman of fifty

looking back into the room
on an occasion I will never know

long after I'm dead

out there
in sexual space

deep in the darkness
breath and rhythm

moving to join
into our orb

how quirky I am
but

I'm not a table
or a pen
or a hill

I'm just a human being
totally representative
as anyone is
outside the self

(and in it)

I wish you would touch me more
it makes me feel happy
and secure

here she comes,
                    down the stairs
slowly, shopping bag in hand

trying not to think
of the heart-beat, the shallow speed
of the breathing

do you listen to your breath

who on earth
tries to control their breath
on their way to the shops

nora's place
nora's place
nora's place
nora's place
nora's place
nora's place
nora's place
nora's place
nora's place
nora's place
nora's place
nora's place
nora's place
nora's place

nora's place
nora's place
nora's place

nora's place nora's place
nora's place nora's place
nora's place nora's place

nora's place nora's
place nora's place
nora's place nora's
place nora's place
nora's place nora's
place nora's place
nora's place nora's
place nora's place
nora's place nora's
place nora's place
nora's place nora's
place nora's place

nora's place nora's place
nora's place nora's place
nora's place nora's place

only this particular
street to walk the length

of, this
is not a metaphor, only

being suddenly
walking down a street

in this place, having
this particular sense
not of anxiety, but

"the fact of the presence of existence"

* *

each time it happens
it seems

that all the intervening times
have disappeared

and this
is all that nora really is

(end of sequence)

Triptych

for those of us
who have to live
outside the
narrative

for those of us
who have to live
outside the
narrative

[illegible]

[illegible]

[illegible] narrative

sequence:

Nine Variations on Larry's Poem

for Larry Butler

What if we, both you and me, were always listening
I mean really listening to the silence – would we hear,
really hear and heed the importance of waiting,
really waiting for the right moment to begin the song.

what if we both
you and me were
always listening
I mean really list-
ening to the silence –

would we hear,
really hear and heed
the importance of wait-
ing, really waiting for

the right moment
to begin the song

What   if we, both you and me,   were always listening
I mean   really listening to the silence –   would we hear,
really hear   and heed the importance   of waiting,
really   waiting for the right moment   to begin the song

what if we
both you and me
were always listening

I mean really listening
to the silence – would we hear,
really hear and heed
the importance of waiting,
really waiting

for the right moment
to begin the song

what if we
both you and me
were always listening

I mean really listening
to the silence – would we hear,
really hear and heed

the importance of waiting,
really waiting
for the right moment

to begin the song

what if
we, both
you and
me were
always
listening
I mean
really list-
ening to
the silence –
would
we hear,
really hear
and heed
the import-
ance of wait-
ing, really
waiting for
the right
moment
to begin
the song

what   if
we   both
you   and
me   were
al   ways
listen   ing
I mean   really
listen-   ing, to

the silence –

would   we
hear,   really
hear   and heed
the   import-
ance   of wait-
ing,   really
waiting   for the
right   moment
to   begin

the song

what importance
to really waiting
were mean always listening
silence
you the heed
if the I and
really would listening
both right
for song to the
we of begin really the

and waiting me hear

what importance
to REALLY **waiting**
were mean *always* *listening*
SILENCE
you the heed
if the I and
really would LISTENING
BOTH right
for SONG to the
we of begin really the

and WAITING me **hear**

( ) ( )
( ) [ ] ( )
( ) ( ) ( ) ( )
[ ]
( ) ( ) ( )
( ) ( ) ( ) ( )
( ) ( ) [ ]
[ ] ( )
( ) [ ] ( ) ( )
( ) ( ) ( ) ( ) ( )

( ) [ ] ( ) ( )

What if we, both you and me, were always listening
I mean really listening to the silence – would we hear,
really hear and heed the importance of waiting,
really waiting for the right moment to begin the song.

(end of sequence)

leaning forward

partly the
inside maybe

the outside
of it, who knows

which
is the which

of it, the real
base line

the hologram
liveable within:

it changes
so readily,

the sense
of

the place
you come

to a constant,
gone, no

coming back
again, maybe

all in the head...

2 Forlorn Poems

(1)

yi keep jist kerryin oan
zif nuthn wuz really

happnin, izif
it wuz aw jist thi wey

it wuz yisstirday an
thi day afore

n it fucks mi up
sumhm awful it

fucks me up
good an proper

n
a think yi know

(2)

cold coventry: a curse

let s/he be a black hole
in some other space;

only another voice
on the phone or
in some other place,

will light my face

walking in the park

am I a spectator at
your sport with yourself

or are we together, as one
sharing the day, under a common sun;

is this a day
in our shared life and time

or you, seen through the hole in the air
that lets my eyes consider you, walking there

beside me . when this is all done
who is to say

what happened this day, whether
sensing your beauty

was just / the echo of nothing
to do with me or the inside of me

but you and your private sense of being
on this another such occasion

not-him

preoccupied with patterns of selfgrowth
                    in a world outside the home
structure, that nexus of self-denial

                        – linking straight
to the arbiters of judgment, the areas
of patriarchal value, beyond the domestic
                        courting

the selfreflective ways
        of becoming / against the emasculated husk
that lurches into alcoholism

that relic of the father, six feet under
        – the counter-organic, the anti-world
that has had it far too good too long

4 football haiku

Bovril Zen

hawf time
n wan hawn clappin
whair the fuck um ah

auld an firm

a blue sky
a green grunn
an a bowl a hatred

playground football

a hawnfu a boays
n two jaickits
three an in

this sporting life

doon three wan
a rid raw wind
nthi ref a bastard

over the moon

a level playing field

at the end of the day

Against Cormorants

for Anne Stevenson

Contextualise the contextualisers!

Give the marginalisers a fair crack of the whip!

Put the victims to the back of the queue! (For that is where we belong.)

Interrogate metaphor and metonymy in the monthly payslip of the person who claims there is no such thing as a person.

A cardinal error: to be forever in conclave, denouncing the canon.

The psychoanalysts of Wordsworth will be recollected in tranquillity.

Does Shakespeare's baldness increase his stature?

Make a witty and provocative case for Adolf Hitler as a neglected German colourist.

They write about poetry as if it had nothing to do with music.

Hark at the presumptuous laughter of the poet. And she hasn't even read Bakhtin on carnival!

Poetry walks barefoot. The only useful critic is a chiropodist.

Trust the poets – not the clerisy. Trust the poems – not the popes.

sequence:

FOODIES

MADE FOR A PEARCE INSTITUTE RESTAURANT EXHIBITION

GOVAN, GLASGOW, JUNE 1996

a could eata hoarss
a hoarss a hoarss
my kingdom furra hoarss

rest assured

the cattle in our pies
were once
professors of psychiatry

oh crumbs
hard cheese

rather a good egg
the royal toast

the day of the triffids
a vegetable plot

Overture "The Scone"

Mendelssohn's Italian Symphony

-------------INTERVAL--------------

Elgar's Vermicelli Concerto

Mahler's Seventh Bagle

✲ ✲ ✲ ✲ ✲ ✲

ah like ma egg turned
the white quite firm

ma yoke saft enough
– though no too runny

thanks a lot

CLINTON IN 'BOILED SWEETIES' PROBE

a gastronomic epaulette :
a chip on the shoulder
an old man's toenail clipping :
a chip off the old bloke
a single European currency :
the Brussels Sprout
what Goethe cried out on his deathbed :
More chips! More chips!

hawfa pakora
is better than
nay samosa

a could go
a right big haddock

deep-fried in batter
crunchy at the tail

thick in the middle
dead white inside

a single fish

GLORIOUS WEATHER IN A TEACUP
TEMPERATURE 90 DEGREES

(end of sequence)

Another Yin, or is it Ane

the inevitable plump, proud,
singer o' sangs

but nary a groiny bit
a distinct absence of rubato

let alone the randy wee heh-heh
of the wee chooky birdy

on its perch here and now

rearguard

who think it will always be
the way they want it to be
not folk like me

losing the rag or
wondering what the fuck

the point of reading
a poetry mag   once again

it seems the battle
not even joined, not even

the conflict
                    recognised

the basis of prosody
still a given, after all these years

as layered text

(Hans Arp: Je Suis un Cheval)

ahma hoarss

ahm oan a train
packt ti thi gunnilz
ma compartmints fuhll
a wummin n ivri seat
a man oan ivri wummins knee
helluva hoat
lik sumhm oot thi tropics
aw thi passengers
fuhlln thir faces
champin away
when thi men aw suddnly girn
they wahnt thir mammy's tit
wahnt thir feed
wahnt thir sook
they oapn thi wummins blouses
lift oot the diddies
sook away fur life
fuhll thimsellz wi good fresh mulk
ahm thi only wan no breastfeedin
n naibdy's sookn it me
n am no sitn oan emdy's knee
an naibdyz sittn oan mine
coz ahma hoarss
sitn straight up a big hoarss
ma hinn legs
upnthi seat
leanin nice n comfy
oan ma front legs
nay bothir a nieeeeeei gh gh gh
oan ma breast six buttns
shiny sixy sex appeal
neat n a row
lik glossy buttns n a uniform
how toaty thi world
how mega its cherries

Tyndale

such was the custom:

led into a ring,
the vestments removed
one by one;

the hands once anointed
scraped
with knife or cut glass;

then the clothes
of a non-priest;

then the strangulation —

the mainstream...

: a clerisy :

coffee, café & the paper

quiet the
habit of

grazing
privately publicly

language /
other-sewn

at one
with the many

sufficing
the day's supply

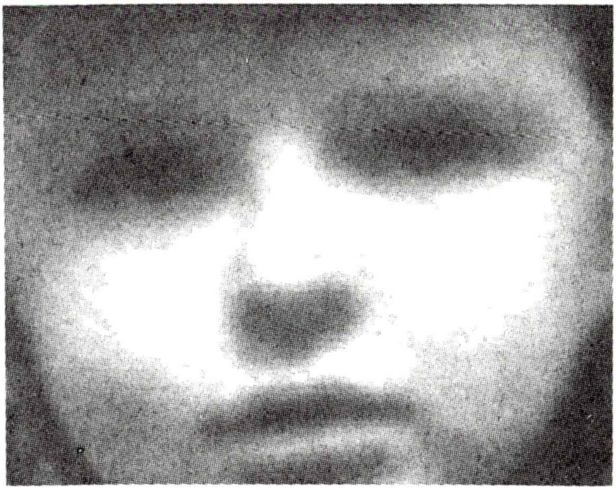

who want
my smile

themselves
their inner child

so to beguile
why

do adults lie

June the Second

it is dawn and my wife is coming to bed
and she has been watching a film about the life of charlie parker

and the air in the bedroom is silent while she undresses
and the light is there at the side of the curtain beyond her head

and she tells me his body gave up of drink and drugs when he was 34
and I decide I am awake and go to the kitchen for a drink of water

and the sky in the north is translucent like a lake
translucent like a lake though it is only 3 am

and when I go back we lightly hold hands as we sometimes do
until the first to be falling asleep begins to twitch and tonight it's Sonya

and I withdraw my hand and lie back looking at the ceiling
I am aged 51 years and nine months and nine to ten days

in hospital

I like seeing nurse frieda knitting
as I like watching my wife knitting
as I liked watching my mother knitting
though she was more of a dabber
(plain and purl, plain and purl)

it's not
"women being in their place"
or knitting the chains that keep them down

just

the future, knitting the future
the present peaceful, quiet
as if

the same woman knitting
for a thousand years

touching your face

with that
silence

it creates
allowing

and
trusting

the allowed;
all that's

been said
and is saying

this time
breath

held
between us

each time
familiar

each time
new

to have access to the silence

to feel part of the silence that is part of that which shares you and not-you

to feel not liable to be attacked at an ontological level

to sense being as not being deprived of being

to sense that it is ok, whatever the it is that is a way of describing you

to sense the it as being something that includes all of your being from the time you were born

to sense the it as being something that includes all of your being from the time you were born

to sense that it is ok, whatever the it is that is a way of describing you

to sense being as not being deprived of being

to feel not liable to be attacked at an ontological level

to feel part of the silence that is part of that which shares you and not-you

to have access to the silence

that each
one be the
subject of
their own
narration

as to
become
verb